## THE DIGS IN

# Escondido Canyon

# THE DIGS IN

# Escondido Canyon

WALTER McDONALD

Texas Tech University Press
Lubbock, Texas

This book was set in 10 1/2 on 15 Baskerville and printed on acid-free paper that meets the guidelines for permanence and durability of the Committee on Production Guidelines for Book Longevity of the Council on Library Resources. ⊗

Designed by Joanna Hill

Manufactured in the United States of America

**Library of Congress Cataloging-in-Publication Data**

McDonald, Walter.
    The digs in Escondido Canyon / Walter McDonald.
      p. cm.
    ISBN 0-89672-258-9 (cloth). — ISBN 0-89672-259-7 (paper)
    I. Title.
    PS3563.A2914D5  1991
    811'.54—dc20                               91-7357
                                                     CIP

91 92 93 94 95 96 97 98 99 / 9 8 7 6 5 4 3 2 1

Texas Tech University Press

Lubbock, Texas 79409-1037 USA

# Acknowledgments

Grateful acknowledgment is made to the following publications in which versions of these poems first appeared, some with different titles:

*America:* "Feeding the Winter Cattle," "Taking Each Deep Breath"
*Berkeley Poetry Review:* "Locket, Where the Water Quit"
*Black Fly Review:* "Caught in a Squall near Pecos"
*Confrontation:* "Combinations"
*De Kalb Literary Arts Journal:* "Reasons for Taking Risks"
*Fiddlehead* (Canada): "Stars and the Laws of Motion"
*Florida Review:* "The Pee Wee Coach"
*Gargoyle:* "Hauling on Hardscrabble"
*Hampden-Sydney Poetry Review:* "With My Father in Winter"
*Kansas Quarterly:* "The Digs in Escondido Canyon"
*Michigan Quarterly Review:* "Sweet Nothings"
*The New Criterion:* "On All Roads Going and Coming"
*New Southern Literary Messenger:* "Eighteen"
*Paris Review:* "Digging on Hardscrabble"
*Poetry Canada Review:* "East of Eden"
*Prism International* (Canada): "One of Our Missiles Is Missing"
*San Jose Studies:* "When It Thunders"
*Sonoma Mandala:* "Home on the Range"
*Threepenny Review:* "Weeds, Barn Owls, All Nibbling Goats"
*Touchstone:* "Two Family Men in Late Summer"
*Windsor Review* (Canada): "Growing Up Near Escondido Canyon"


"Hawks in a Bitter Blizzard" and "The Goats of Summer" were first published in the *Atlantic,* copyright 1989 and 1990. "The Winter Before the War" was first published in the *Kenyon Review,* copyright 1987. "Father's Straight Razor" and "Starting a Pasture" were first published in *Poetry,* copyright 1990 the Modern Poetry Association. "Hunting the Pasture," "Mercy and the Brazos River," and "Praying for More than Thunder" reprinted from *Prairie Schooner,* by permission of University of Nebraska Press; copyright 1988, 1991 University of Nebraska Press.


I'm especially grateful to the National Endowment for the Arts for a fellowship, which provided the time to write many of these poems.

for the children

# Contents

## 3. Taking Each Deep Breath

# 1

## THE GOATS

## OF SUMMER

# The Barn on the Farm We're Buying

We slide the barn door wide and cough.  Dust swarms,
the half-buried droppings of horses and owls
like feather dusters uncleaned for decades.
The rattle of rollers echoes in the barn,
abandoned to straw never changed.  Hames of horses

creak when we lift them.  Our flashlights
sweep past empty stalls.  Dust floats
from every beam, embalming all but us.
Not even a barn owl stares, digesting
last night's mice.  We tap the walls,

the sturdy posts.  Why do we talk hardly above
a whisper, when no one's close enough to hear
and we hold the deed?  Did he care
strangers would buy his barn
when he and his horses were gone?

Where are the rotten planks
we'd counted on, the cracked rafters,
the sagging roof?  How can we tear down walls
he built to last?  Where are the layers
of gauze cobwebs we thought would serve

as kindling?  On these dry plains,
can't even spiders live?  Nothing in the barn
seems old but leather, and dust
we're growing used to, our other odor,
the earth we're beginning to call home.

# The Goats of Summer

The clink of steel diggers rammed
on sandstone makes pet goats easy to despise.
Without a fence, they'd baaa and billy leap
wet fields of oats or cotton, nothing sacred

to their hooves and nibbling lips.
Leaning the diggers in a hole of stubborn rock,
I wipe a wet bandana on my face
and sling my Stetson like a watering can.

Standing still at noon, I feel my boot soles burn.
What madness made me believe the silly song
of barkers selling goats, kids for kids,
the catchy phrase erasing the smell

of pellets, the wide-eyed grin of baby goats
and children tugging my sleeve
more whimsy than a man could stand.
So now, days later, where are they,

those knee-high babies nudging for bottles?
What are these hip-high goats with deep voices,
butting the back yard gate until it warps?
Where are my kids who promised to clean

the daily straw reeking like Noah's privy?
Tugging old leather gloves back on,
pliable with sweat like second skin,
I lift the double blades and drive them down

like breaking teeth, squeeze out the broken stone
and go on digging, rolls of barbed wire
waiting to be strung, a dozen more dry holes
before there'll be some order to this dirt.

# Mercy and the Brazos River

My great-greats came to hardscrabble plains
when a dollar an acre was outrage. Quakers
from Iowa, they listened for God's still voice
in sandstorms, a silence under stars.
Patient, they waited for their hearts
to lead them over prairie sprawled flat
around them, a thousand miles of parchment

under the will of heaven. No trees grew native,
only buffalo grass tall enough to hold the bones
of slaughtered buffalos. If they hoped for angels
to wrestle for crops in the desert, when they found
this winding Texas stream, *Rio de los Brazos
del Dios*, they believed. Now, that canyon's
drained after decades of irrigation,

near a city of a quarter million
which pumps its gyppy water
from a lake a hundred miles away. In 1880,
the dugout where they huddled all winter
was a tent half buried in walls of white caliche.
In spite of rattlesnakes and drought,
they called it home.

The holes of prairie dogs pocked every acre.
Even the home they dug uprooted a colony of dogs.
They plugged the burrows and settled down
to stay, enough grass like pastures of heaven
for cows which survived the blizzards.
I've seen the grainy photographs,
held in my hands their beaten plows.

How could they leave their families for this?
What did they hope for, choking down rabbits
and snakes, enduring wind from wide horizons
without one tree, nothing but hawks in the sky
and slow whirlpools of buzzards? I've heard
the first deep well they dug was hopeless,
every dry foot like stone, and the second.

Before the third well struck an aquifer
at last, they turned enough prairie under
for a crop and a baby's grave, their plow
silver-shiny, their wagon broken often
but repaired in time to bump down that steep
caliche canyon and haul back barrels of water
from the river of the arms of God.

# The Digs in Escondido Canyon

Last night the Brazos froze. The trucks are here,
bulldozers waiting for the sun. Foremen rise up
for work, fresh coffee all the history they need.
Fish scales glisten through ice like mica.
A dry caliche cutbank shelters Uncle Claude,

something to pitch chips on and worship,
huddled. The pale flames waver like ghosts
of tribes drawn to this stream ten thousand years
before railroad trestles and beef. A million years
to cut a canyon through the plains, forty to pump it dry.

Now, like Moses we walk across the Brazos on dry land.
This fork once watered coyotes and wolves,
bears big as buffalos. He's scraped this dust
for skulls and arrows all his life, uncovered
mammoth tusks and fangs, the pelvic bones of women.

This mud's a genealogy. And now they'd dam it,
hoard this trickle when it thaws, flood miles
of pottery under a lake that's necessary—he knows,
he knows, good water's gold. But they'd bury
natives who worshipped the same tornado skies

we worship. Over his live body: they'll have to pour
their tons of concrete over him, to shut him up,
or tear down his flag and haul him off to jail,
a harmless drudge who means nobody harm, who only means
to dig for bones he might have loved.

# Growing Up Near Escondido Canyon

With bristles and picks
precise as diamond cutters,
they chip two hundred years a day,
tagging snake bones and buffalos, bowls
and amulets of teeth.

Here in caliche they've found five flints
buried twelve thousand years,
nothing on either side for centuries
as if they killed each other off,
not even small-boned rabbits,

layer after layer like diamonds
malleted at bad angles and shattered.
Growing up a mile from here,
I raced my brother
over flat plains,

hawks on bent wings
gawking at us, dipping and sidling
on summer thermals.
Years before diggers climbed down
these cliffs, we made up lies

at night—murders, something moaning
across the canyon, bodies
buried in shallow graves,
dug up by dogs and eaten.
My brother found the bones.

In moonlight, trying not to shiver,
afraid our father would catch us
sneaking home,
we huddled by a stick fire
cursing, smoking bark cigars.

Midnight, thinking of what we'd found,
we held them up to the moon,
cow bones or coyotes'
we believed were human,
turning them over and over.

# Feeding the Winter Cattle

We lifted bales and dropped them heavy
from the wagon.  Hay burst like melons,
even on a cushion of snow.  Plodding,

a bossy cow took charge of each split bale,
head down, her long horns hooking air,
her purple tongue sucking the bale like a melon.

Dumbly, the others followed, bobbing their heavy heads.
Stark sunshine made me squint, watching a hawk
rising on thermals.  The dogs weaved behind the wagon,

panting, sniffing for tracks, wetting the wagon
when it stopped.  The mules didn't care,
stubborn as if asleep in their harness.

Grandpa coaxed, "Please, sir, Big Ed.
Once more for daddy, Lou," tapping black reins
like a love pat.  And bump, we'd lurch again,

my little brother and I grabbing for balance
on floor boards slick with straw,
stabbing our gloves into another bale

and lifting, heaving it over like ballast
between the dogs, like another Christmas visit
dropping away forever.

# Boys and the Laws of Mercy

Under the hat racks, under the drip
of plastic raincoats, I showed Billy Ray
the bat, huddled by rain boots, wings folded
like a cape, nose like a puppy's.
Billy Ray pulled off his shoe
and scooped it. The eyes, the throbbing throat

gave it away, limp and wheezing,
a hole in its breast like buckshot.
It must have flown through a door
like a cave, wobbling through halls
to our room. Billy Ray and I took turns
stroking the fur, the ears that twitched

when we touched them. After someone told
the teacher, before the rest came running,
it simply died. Billy Ray lifted it
in his hand and stood there
squeezing his shoe
and daring anyone to laugh.

# Digging on Hardscrabble

In a deep well I swung a pickax
into packed caliche, so dark I aimed the ax
by feel. My brother leaned back safe
away from me. Sweat was a blessing
the body gave. My brother called out
and drank, metal canteens the only
water we might find. I sank down
to my knees, baptized myself

and drank, more soothing to my back
than to my tongue. If dirt walls cracked,
we could be buried with salamanders
after years of drought. Better clay than this
had crumbled, one cousin crushed
when I was nine—Daingerfield, pine country,
black dirt heaped higher than my head.
But here we were on parched

hardscrabble plains, digging for water
the old way. A traveling dowser
rambled over our acres and pointed,
his quivering sycamore stick
bone dry and hollow at the core.
And though we knew three wells out of four
are sand, this was our fourth.
Kneeling, nearing the limit of our hour,

I groped for the shovel, scooped fast
to fill the bucket, and tugged.
Faces we loved looked down
from up above and reeled, the creak
and clatter of rope and pulley. I drained
the last canteen, then reached for the rope
and sent my brother up, spinning
into almost liquid light.

# The Winter Before the War

One winter, sledgehammers couldn't break ice
cloudy in the troughs.  For days we rode for cattle
frozen where they fell, some huddled by barbed wire,
stumbling in snowdrifts, sheeted with ice

like armor.  Sundown, herding survivors home,
we passed a playa lake frozen hard, one whiteface bull
caught in the center.  The bull had broken through
up to his horns, his tail raised like a flag,

his head on a platter of ice, wide muzzle stiff
as if he had frozen bawling.  That night, we fed
the lucky steers and barred the corral to save them.
At supper, we smoked in the bunkhouse and played poker

and argued how long a bull could have bawled
when the lake gave way.  We flipped our cards
and drank and cursed our luck, and tried to ignore
stiff wind and shingles banging overhead.

# Sweet Nothings

The same old songs keep twanging back,
slurred by steel guitars and a fiddle,
tear honey for the heart. They make me young

and vulnerable again, for three minutes,
as if Saigon never happened.
Honky-tonk darlings saved us

from killing each other, gored
and stomped on all week, stubborn
as the bulls we rode, trying to ignore

the TV war. Good-hearted women led us
to the dance floor, waltzing to slow sad songs
and humming. After the last good waltz,

sipping cold Lone Star after midnight,
we glowered at men too old for the draft
doing a fast fox-trot on the sawdust.

We stared through blue smoke layered
like gunfire, slouched with hollow cans
crushed easy in our fists.

# Caught in a Squall Near Pecos

We listen to hail waste itself
on shale and cactus, rain rushing
in gullies to the creek bed.
Cramped in a cave
we share with snakes and scorpions,

we rub beads off the barrels
of our rifles, ready to throw down
on bobcats.  Our boots
shove a ring of campfire stones
so old the soot is glazed.

Whoever listens to rain in a cave believes
he knows how it was, craves fire
in a hearth, marks his claim
with boot heels deep in caliche
as if sandstone were granite.

Here for an hour, he stacks stones
wide enough for years and digs
for matches, torching his handkerchief,
hunting map, the butt ends of limbs
dragged from the ashes.

After the cloudburst, hail melts fast
in hardpan heat.  We crawl out
and leave live coals
as if we aim to return
with whatever meat we're after.

# Weeds, Barn Owls, All Nibbling Goats

We chop these weeds with hoes filed shiny.
Nothing but rain could save these puny roots.
Enough of killing weeds for a hobby. Wrong,
maybe, trying to make loose sand
say beans as well as grass, the nearest lake

a hundred miles away. Bless weeds
that wring hard water from this dirt.
We'll throw the gate wide open
and let goats graze until they bloat.
Even a stunted pasture feeds them.

The days of miracles may not be gone.
Too old to start over, we watch for signs,
a front, a steady shower. An inch
would yield Kentucky Wonder beans to freeze.
Neighbors could pick their fill.

Even that dried-up playa lake
could be a pond. We could breed ducks
imported from swamps. Afternoons,
we rock together on the back porch,
sipping iced tea from depression glass,

watching the flat mirages for a hawk,
the shimmer of heat waves breeding
whirlwinds but no angels in the clouds,
sometimes an owl blinded by sunlight,
weaving from barn to barn.

# 2

## THE CALL OF ALL

## THINGS COMMON

# The Pee Wee Coach

I ring the doorbell and wait, cap on my head
and grinning. They open the storm door wide,
believing my T-shirt, my pocket tucks,
the lineups and plays on my clipboard.

They hope I'll prove I'm good, so I shake hands
with both, as if baseball's an exclusive
summer camp and I'm here to see if her little one
is worthy. The kid comes out, skinny and short,

or fat, nothing at six hinting baseball but his Keds.
If he whines, clings to his mother or won't talk,
I put him in right field where he'll be safe
to dream and pinch himself and pee. I say

I'm proud to have him, and practice is at four.
I field their questions, legs wide apart,
clipboard crossed on my chest as if I know
secrets of how their son can bat .400.

I give the talk about how baseball's not
just playing hard and winning, but having fun
and learning to be men. But I drop hints
of titles the teams I've coached have won,

the names of boys I've helped win scholarships
to college. I say I feel we've got the boys
to win the pennant. By then they're ready
for sweat and tears, or sitting on the bench

if that will do it—all but the boy,
who sees me as I am, a man with a stopwatch
on his wrist, hairy, selling something
to his folks, a coach who probably has boys

already picked to play, guys who can hit
and spit and tell jokes about his sisters
and his mother, the things it takes
to be a big boy in the world.

# Reasons for Taking Risks

Not when the nose comes up
and we think we'll die climbing,
but later, the second we glimpse
clouds tumble over wing tips

is time to shove the rudder and chase
the propeller to a stalled arc
like the curved claws of a hammer,
a violent hammerhead stall,

slicing back down through
a vertical coil of the prop wash.
Pilots mad enough to stress wing spars
and blood learn where the sky ends

is earth. Then off again
into clear unstable air, risking
nothing that lasts in climbs and loops
up to the sun, the wild blue.

# Combinations

Hot hands build gimbals steady
for rough seas, feel tumblers fall
in combination locks.
Hot hands stack any deck.

Down to our last dime,
we learn where to kick a jukebox,
how to twist a tightwad vending machine
to its knees. We learn how hard

to push for a raise, a fight,
a divorce date. We code computers
and poker faces so no one
can crash our secret hearts.

# One of Our Missiles Is Missing

All bets, all unnecessary breaths
are canceled.  Awaiting transport,

a pilgrim swallows blue flames
in a roadhouse.  Walling a well,

a man soon to be married
finds in the silt a shark's tooth

buried a million years.
Bats in a cavern

squeeze the belly of heaven
and swing like bells.

# East of Eden

Eve's firstborn fed the snake for years,
foxes he snared in his fields,
saving rabbits in pits for the snake
to swallow like grapes. Cain hated
sheep and goats, crows which ate
his struggling grain, almost a garden.

Cain blamed his parents for cursing him
with a brother who raised flocks
which foraged all green leaves.
He never blamed the snake,
which had ripe apples for any mood,
which understood the highs and lows

of a man whose parents were fools.
When Eve tried to warn him, Cain
beat his ears, called his mother bitch,
inventing names like his father.
The snake coiled safely on a stone
behind him, sticking its tongue out at Eve

and hissing. Cain went insane with labor,
hauling off stones, forcing a desert to say leaves
as well as thorns, digging canals
to save his dying crops. At harvest,
Cain offered to burn his golden wheat,
begging his way back to gardens without rocks

and scorpions, without drought.
The snake said, Fool, God's thunder hovers
like a dove over that stinking valley
of shadows, where your lazy brother
raises goats. Pick up this stone:
you'll think of something.

# On All Roads Going and Coming

That girl in the album sharpened hoes
as if dead weeds could save her. That was my sister
when we were ten and seventeen. At night
she studied Greek, not even trying to resist
the tug of wings, somewhere to fly to from plains
so flat she wept. She studied maps like code.

Wherever her finger fell was magic. She grabbed
and shook me like a doll, demanded why our great-
grandparents crossed a prairie. Why
did they break down in wagons, trapped
between a dry caliche canyon and the Alps.
She stared at army planes from the airfield,

all of them going somewhere, if only to war.
Now, she's off again somewhere. She's been
to Athens, reads six other tongues than Greek.
Her children left home one by one, flung wide
like Texas stars. She sold her title to the farm
and lives in town. After each trip,

she swears she'll let blue skies be empty.
Her garden sprawls while she's away,
but she won't let me touch it, won't hire
a yardman to save her weeds from scorn.
For days when she returns she rakes the leaves
and burns them, heaping them high.

# Eighteen

I cannot bring him back.
He has too many scars
to be a child again.
His knuckles have been crushed,
rebuilt, and crushed again.

Blood is father to the bones
of man, pleading *patience,
patience.* He leads too often
with his right. Holding him
on my lap, I taught him

patty-cake, cat's cradle,
how to open the door
and see all the people, then
how to walk, how to make fire,
how to bed down under stars.

# The Call of All Things Common

*We are called human*
Richard Hugo

That part of me that needs a mob
comes back in edited Beijing footage—
raised fists, the common squalor of mats
and empty fruit juice cans, the noise
of ordinary voices. This was no Halloween charade,
a place for masks. What haunts me most

is not the myth of easy overthrow
like two-hour movies in my living room,
not bullhorn calls to honor, not even one
bold dancer before the tanks,
like the Poles riding stallions
against steel Nazi panzers.

I think of scenes bounced back from space,
those close-up eyes in crowds
of thousands, aware of children
they hope to raise someday, braving
cameras mounted on every corner,
recording everything.

# Father's Straight Razor

This old razor loves a beard, the subtle
scrape of flesh all it asks for.
It glides the moist, soaped stubble
like a water spider, sharp enough
to puncture flesh, balanced on the stretched
surface tension of skin.

I remember its touch along my jaw,
the cold Toledo steel slicing me
squeegee clean, before I grew a beard.
Unfolded, sharpened back and forth
on my father's stiff, black leather strop,
it smoothed my honeymoon face twice daily,

leaving no shadow to burn my bride.
I remember my father's face when I flew home
after his attack, the nights in CCU,
the first wave of his hand, his last request,
to shave him before he saw Mother.
I remember his eyes barely wavering,

his scalp buried in the pillow,
exposing the slack stretch of his face,
when I touched him, the soft prickle of a week's
white growth under my nervous thumb
and fingers, the willing tilt of his chin,
the short, slick flicks of the blade

on his throat and jaw, floating
over his blue-veined skin and bone, his face
coming clean and true through the lather,
my own eyes barely wavering, like nothing
I'd ever get to do again, nothing
I wouldn't have done to save him.

# 3

TAKING EACH

DEEP BREATH

# Two Family Men in Late Summer

From cove to cove we troll
through water bugs wading waves.

We coast under oaks and ship the oars
by stumps white as skulls, nodding, this one,

this one, trusting mesquite and sumac
along the bank, hives of mistletoe

eating the live oaks. We have faith
in water, in our fingers' hooked nerves

fumbling striped and speckled plugs,
in lily pads hiding trunks

sunk longer than we've lived.
On a dammed lake we flip our lures

beyond stumps, braced for the sudden
snap of the rod tip.

# Locket, Where the Water Quit

This town is like a brother
broken by the war.  Never mind which war,
it's haunted.  The school is boarded up.
Farmers who kept the stores in business
died or lost their fields at auction.

The Ogallala aquifer dried up
under the southern third of the county,
plains where it rains two times a year.
Hired hands who guard the bankers' herds
drive now to Lubbock—an enclosed mall,

flea markets, a thousand fast-food shops.
Hunters with guns already loaded
come through the town for gas and Cokes,
joke about a town only cock pheasants
keep on the map.  The old man

who takes their credit cards and quarters
still gives away too much,
gives us the sad complaints he always told
like the same old country and western
songs sobbing on his jukebox.

Tumbleweeds each fall bounce into town
like motorbikes with sidecars, drivers
drunk, careening down the town's one road.
The wind invades and empty houses let them.
Windows we wanted to smash as kids

are smashed.  We wonder when.
No matter where we've been, it's home.
Except for the one store holding on,
nobody's here, the whole town occupied
by ghosts showing surprising gestures

of defiance—trimmed shrubs,
fresh-painted porch swings hanging straight,
garage doors down, flags raised
on mailboxes disguised as plows
and irrigation pipes.

# When It Thunders

At night we flash back
to the mountains, when we hear thunder.
Curtains aside, we see stiff  lightning

in clouds looming like peaks.
For seconds, we're young again,
the air thinner in the rain.

It seldom showers here
where we live on flat plains
fenced by barbed wire.

Thunderstorms tumble
far away in the east
down arroyos.  Darkness,

a million stars.  The only sounds
the ceiling fan, coyotes,
your deep, familiar breath.

# Starting a Pasture

Flooded with sun, this ranch looks like a rice field,
a trick of optics. Rattlers roam boldly
because their world is dust, natives as foreign
to our ways as wolves which disappeared by 1880.
Surviving coyotes sway in ballets for the moon,
heads back, worshipping only heaven. We mete out mice
to cats and owls, fat on our grain sacked up for cattle.

Stuttering owls cough softly in our sleep
like goats, another herd we're saving. Neighbors
drive slowly by and stare, their windows tight.
They scoff, although we're feeding thousands,
*cabrito* and Texas mutton worth more than beef.
Let them laugh while little bells lead lambs and goats
to market. All week we find our cows, heads down,

praying to all the stubble they own. We fill their troughs
and call, and they come floating through a lake
of shimmering sunlight. My wife's green eyes
play homespun when the chores are done, better chords
than fiddles and sweet guitars. After a rain,
fat cattle wade alfalfa ankle deep. It's grain,
not shade, hot cattle need. Often in our fields

I find buzzards, too late to save a calf
I would have gladly fed.  My sons ride the range
to keep them airborne, gliding on thermals.
I hate tornadoes and slow whirlpools of wings.
Don't look, I say, as if blind luck could save us.
Let cattle claim our pastures, let lambs turn into wool,
let buzzards wait for city dogs tossed out of cars.

This morning in the field I found another tow sack
full of kittens.  They'll grow up gladly in our barn,
making the owls work harder for their mice, saving our wheat
for export.  All winter we sow alfalfa for livestock,
two of each kind in a starving world, buffalos
imported from Wyoming, a flock of ostriches which came
last night by train, wide eyed and panting.

# Home on the Range

Sandstorms kept my mother inside,
heavy with me, pinning blankets
to windows to dampen dust
she was afraid would choke us.

Same flat horizon, same
sandy miles to the mountains:
home is more than a state of mind.
It's grit in your teeth,

wrinkles you put in the sheets,
an old dog limping
you alone must decide
when to put to sleep.

# Hauling on Hardscrabble

Driving fast, I watch fence posts
funnel more than road—call it warp,
a trick of optics—more posts flashing by

than a man could dig a day. I remember years ago,
before Saigon, buzzing on training flights
ten feet above the dirt, five hundred knots.

I heard the navigator hush. Cactus and pale mesquites
rushed underneath, a blur. Our wing tips in seconds
crossed miles of barbed-wire plains.

A hawk flashed by, a flick of a glimpse.
The stunned steers never looked up, gone
before they heard us. I held it low,

the prairie a bowl enclosing us,
a blur of dust. I lifted the nose at last
and climbed, and heard the navigator sigh.

I saw steers and windmills fall sharply away,
the prairie caught in its peaceful spiral—
barbed wires and drought, flash floods,

wind-spinning vanes and water trickling
from the pipes, the constant trudge of fat,
trapped cattle grazing behind barbed wires.

Even now, when I slow the rig
with air brakes, they never look up,
not even when I turn slowly

down a narrow lane between pastures,
not even when I back this empty truck
tight against the loading dock.

# Praying for More than Thunder

Trapped on the plains, we dream
of trout snapping the dawn hatch,
starving for flies we tied all winter.

All year we practice witching
with our rods, like Aaron's
which budded without touching dirt.

Nothing but rain can save us—
seed in the planters for weeks,
drilled by faith into hardpan,

all of us cursing like sailors
Christ, for small rains down to rain,
a plague of locusts, lightning

to strike our barns, or floods
to force us to the mountains.
We would mortgage our plows

and start again in the Rockies,
but who can drive away from dirt
when white thunderclouds

mushroom each noon to tempt us,
but disappear by dusk. We would
sell our own fields for thunder.

# Hunting the Pasture

They've done it again, gutshot a cow
in the pasture.  Signs don't stop them,
miles from the nearest land leased for hunting.

At night we might forgive someone
trespassing barbed-wire brush
and spooked, stalking a wild hope

of stumbling on antlers, shooting
when something slides by his boots.
Whoever climbs a fence in sunlight risks more

than fangs.  If she feels us kneeling,
blood muzzles her.  Her bossy eyes glaze
on a distant mesa, her black barrel heaves.

# The Last Five Acres of Timber

They've cut our last trees down, loblolly pines
the color of money. We take the sun for granted
on the plains. Empty sunlight cheapens pine sap
heady as a mountain still. We wade through stumps

and kick old trunks, pines which died on their own.
They poof like toadstools, dust to dust.
They'll rise again as seedlings, too late for us,
all bark we own killed by ten million beetles,

condemned, flames the only way to save infested acres.
Rangers faithful to their tasks have bulldozed
stacks of logs, a slash-and-burn salvation.
Each fall we drive from Texas to trees more costly

than the cash they earn, leased to loggers.
We've waged this tree-house dream for years. Our children
pretended goats were ours. Little bells led goats
to pasture through these woods, a neighbor's herd.

Now stumps are ours, and fungus. The birds
are gone, the men who felled the logs are home.
Silence stuns us, after the whine of chain saws.
Men who'll burn the logs are miles away in smoky bars,

planning tomorrow's fire storm, the best way
to torch them all—the fallen logs and mushrooms,
scallions and truffles, down to the lowest
burning bush, the last miraculous tree.

# Hawks in a Bitter Blizzard

Hard work alone can't drive blue northers off.
Nine blizzards out of ten blow out
by Amarillo, nothing this far south

but flakes and a breeze to make a man
in shirt sleeves shiver. Every few years,
Canada roars down, fast-freezing cattle

in the fields, dogs caught between barns,
hawks baffled on fence posts. Stubborn,
hawks refuse to hunker down in burrows

with drowsy rattlesnakes and rabbits.
They drown in their own breath bubbles,
crystal as the sheen on barbed wires

freezing in the rain. Wood carvers driving by,
grinding on chains down icy roads,
see them at dawn and envy, tempted

to haul the fence posts home and burn them,
nothing in oak or juniper they carve
ever as wild and staring as those eyes.

# With My Father in Winter

We hiked through woods to pools
I believed no one but he
could find.  He knew all trees
by faith, never glanced back,
his fly line flipping fast
under aspens, the fly
flicking upstream to pools
no wider than his rod.
His eyes searched eddies
and stones for cutthroats
shimmering deep in currents
sapphire cold.

Now, geese overhead
aim north, and somewhere
a hooked trout flounces.
Even here among these stones,
in snow, I hear it splash.
On a stiff green carpet,
I stand bundled like a boy
under a flapping canopy
and stare at black mud
frozen in chunks
while someone's words
flick out across a hole.

# Stars and the Laws of Motion

These trees yield networks of buds,
like the expanding universe.
Stars we believe true for navigation
and love are constantly unfaithful,
flung forever outward

toward black holes. Computers predict
in a million years Orion's stars
will be like the scorpion
that stalks him, his straight belt
bowed into legs, the stars which were his sword

raised like a stinger. Years back,
we knew an ocean, jellyfish
like blue phosphorus balloons
bobbing ashore and dying. Sea gulls
scattered above us like ghosts, moon-gray

and silent, like memories of others
we've loved and left, when it was over.
Tonight, after weeding the garden,
we rest in lawn chairs under stars
vanishing at the speed of light.

# Leaving the Middle Years

Slow blues beckon us to move,
the sawdust dance floor almost deserted.
Sunday morning fog won't settle outside
for hours, though it has already here,

lazy smoke layered like haze
in the mellow glow of the jukebox.
We wonder where our children are tonight,
flung wide from coast to coast,

old enough to choose their own
curfew and music. We miss them
and their own sweet babies growing
fast as these wax records spinning

on a vintage burly Wurlitzer
not even as old as us. Come,
let's join sad others on the dance floor
before it closes, the whine and glide

of fiddles and steel guitars
sentimental enough for lovers bound
by more than rings and wrinkles
deeper than any scars.

# Taking Each Deep Breath

Rain, the long arm of thunder, reaches us
at last.  After months of drought
and shimmering mirage, so much staccato fuss
to make one pond.  Steers wade the pasture

and stare, lower broad muzzles into floating grass
and shut their eyes, and why not,
about to be hauled off in trucks when the rain stops.
Propped on the back porch, smoking,

we watch a prairie fade in a squall line,
hard rain like the days of Noah.  The breeze
is fresh honey in the hive.  We are two bees
in a pasture.  The steers go under in the haze,

even the barn, only this porch swing
dry in the downpour, an ark we rock on,
gliding under the crack of thunder,
taking each deep breath to let it go.

# Books by Walter McDonald

*Poetry*

The Digs in Escondido Canyon
Night Landings
After the Noise of Saigon
Rafting the Brazos
Splitting Wood for Winter
The Flying Dutchman
Witching on Hardscrabble
Burning the Fence
Working Against Time
Anything, Anything
One Things Leads to Another
Caliban in Blue

*Fiction*

A Band of Brothers: Stories from Vietnam